People and Nature

Program Authors

Connie Juel, Ph.D.

Jeanne R. Paratore, Ed.D.

Deborah Simmons, Ph.D.

Sharon Vaughn, Ph.D.

ISBN: 0-328-21488-4
Copyright © 2008 Pearson Education, Inc.

9 10 V011 12 11 10 09 08
CC1

PEARSON

Scott
Foresman

Editorial Offices: Glenview, Illinois • Parsippany, New Jersey • New York, New York
Sales Offices: Boston, Massachusetts • Duluth, Georgia • Glenview, Illinois
Coppell, Texas • Sacramento, California • Mesa, Arizona

People and Nature

Green Thumbs in Action

What's so great about gardens?

NATURE
The True Story

How do people explain nature?

Green Thumbs in Action

Contents

Green Thumbs in Action

Words 2 the Wise

Gardens have been around for a long time. Why do so many people like them? Think about this as you read.

Let's Explore

Gardens

People around the world like gardens. Gardens are nice to look at. We can visit a few gardens now. That will help us see what can grow in a garden.

Vegetable Gardens

Yummy things to eat grow in some gardens. Which vegetables do you like? Corn? Beans? Peas? You can grow them in a vegetable garden. People plant these gardens to get fresh vegetables and feed their families. Many people plant vegetables in spring. Then they can eat fresh vegetables all summer long.

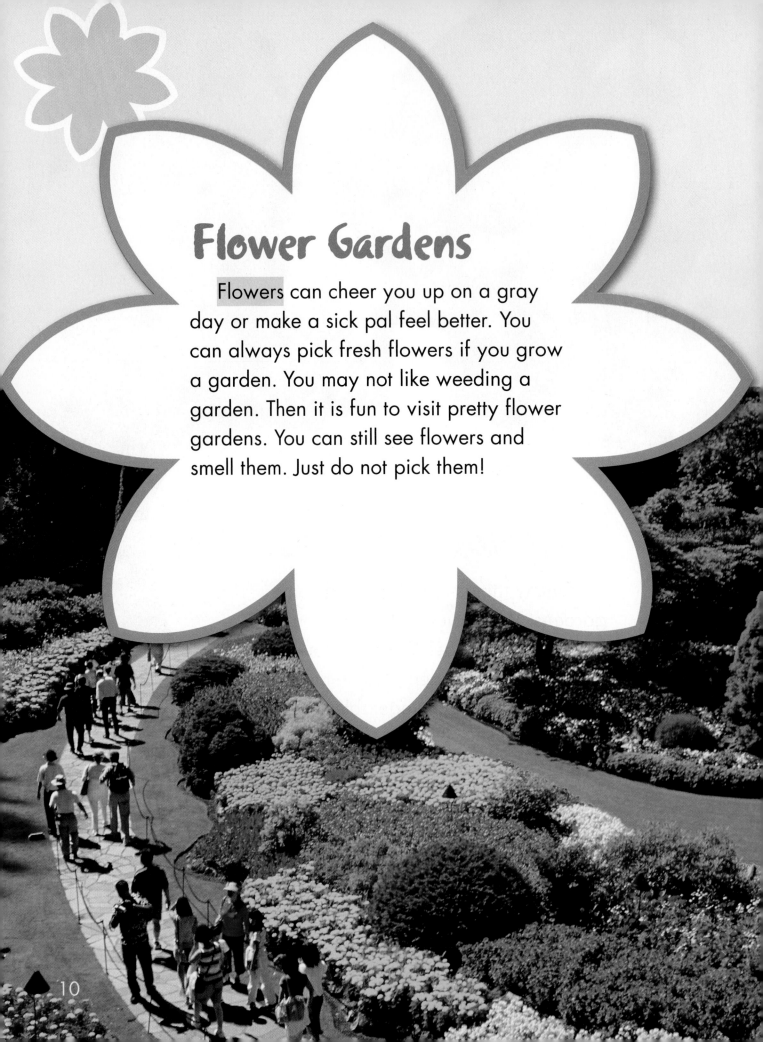

Flower Gardens

Flowers can cheer you up on a gray day or make a sick pal feel better. You can always pick fresh flowers if you grow a garden. You may not like weeding a garden. Then it is fun to visit pretty flower gardens. You can still see flowers and smell them. Just do not pick them!

Rock Gardens

Have you ever seen big rocks between flowers on a hill? You may also see a stream or pond there. This is a rock garden. A rock garden is not a garden where rocks grow. It is a garden where rocks help make the garden look pretty.

Gardens grow in many places. You do not need a big space. Just find a bit of soil, scatter some seeds, and get started.

GARDENS
Past and Present

by Bret Allan

Let's look at some gardens people have planted from the past to the present.

The Hanging Gardens of Babylon*

Babylon was a city in a desert 2,500 years ago. It is hard to grow plants in a desert. The soil isn't rich.** The weather is dry. It doesn't rain much. But long ago, people in that desert made gardens grow.

*Babylon (BAB-uh-lon) This city from long ago was on land that is now part of the country of Iraq.

**rich good for growing plants

How did they do it? They put the Hanging Gardens on the banks, or sides, of a river. And they planted them on different levels.* Ropes lifted buckets of water from the river up to the top level. Then the water ran down to other levels. That's how the plants got plenty of water.

Many people back then wrote about these gardens. That is why we know about them today.

*levels layers or steps

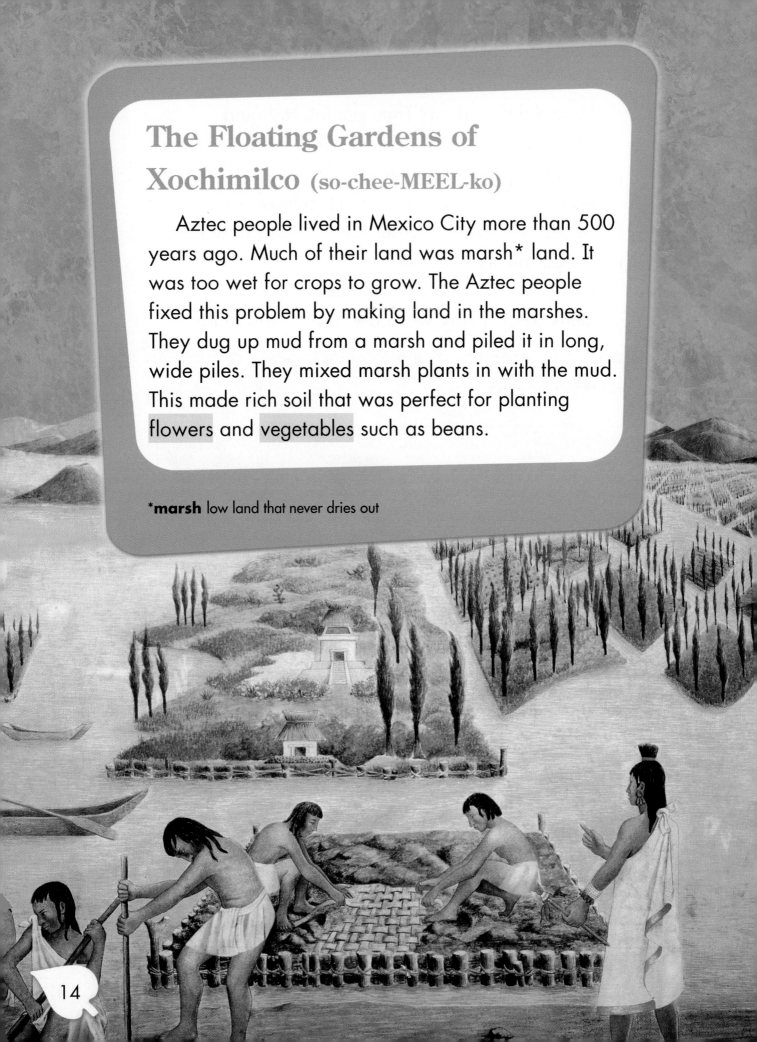

The Floating Gardens of Xochimilco (so-chee-MEEL-ko)

Aztec people lived in Mexico City more than 500 years ago. Much of their land was marsh* land. It was too wet for crops to grow. The Aztec people fixed this problem by making land in the marshes. They dug up mud from a marsh and piled it in long, wide piles. They mixed marsh plants in with the mud. This made rich soil that was perfect for planting flowers and vegetables such as beans.

*marsh low land that never dries out

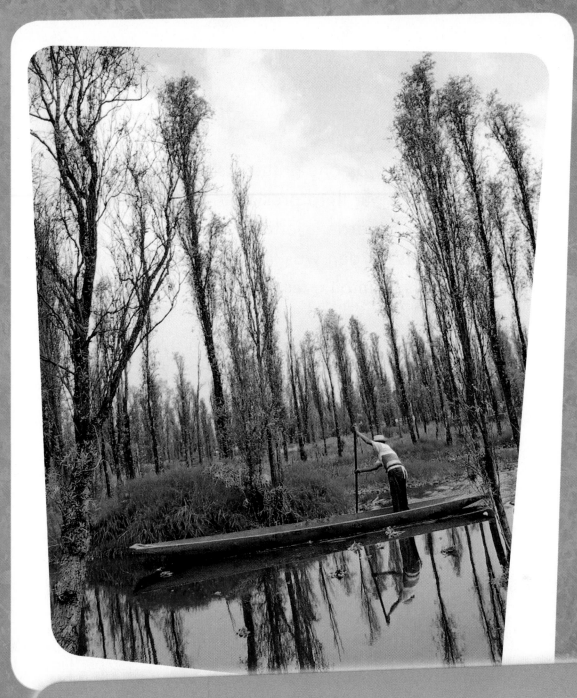

Aztec people often made homes on these piles of soil. This made it easy for them to tend* crops. It was also easy to keep the soil wet with marsh water so close by. Today people still grow flowers and vegetables for Mexico City in these gardens.

*tend care for

Monticello*

Thomas Jefferson was one of the first leaders of our country. He was our third president. But Jefferson also liked growing a garden. Jefferson made notes that tell us what his garden was like. He planted flowers and plants from all over the world.

*__Monticello__ (mon-tuh-CHEL-o) Thomas Jefferson's home in Virginia

Jefferson planted more than 150 kinds of apples, peaches, and grapes. His gardens held 300 kinds of vegetables. And did you know that Jefferson really liked peas a lot? In his garden, he had fifteen kinds of peas!

People still visit his home and gardens. They can learn what gardens were like in Jefferson's day.

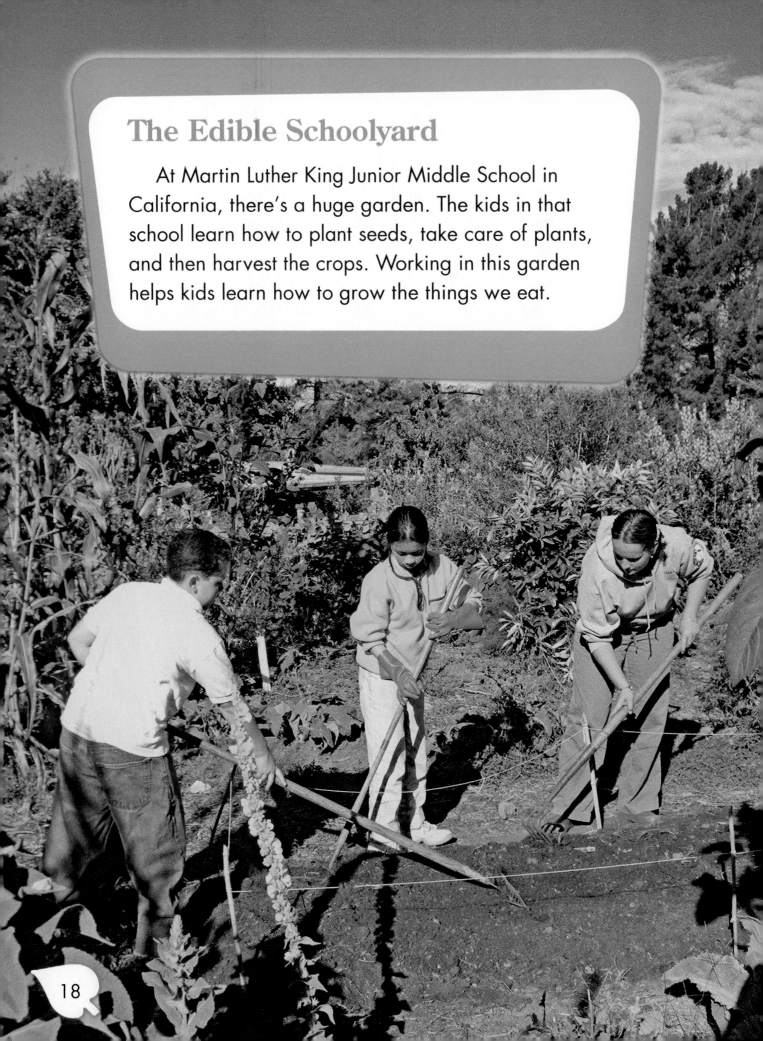

The Edible Schoolyard

At Martin Luther King Junior Middle School in California, there's a huge garden. The kids in that school learn how to plant seeds, take care of plants, and then harvest the crops. Working in this garden helps kids learn how to grow the things we eat.

When it's time to pick the vegetables, there are yummy things, like peas, to snack on. But their work isn't over yet. Next, the kids use vegetables from the garden to prepare meals. Then they eat the meal together. When lunch is over, the scraps go back in the soil. This keeps the soil rich for next year's garden.

What Do You Think?

In the gardens you read about, what steps did people take to grow their flowers and vegetables?

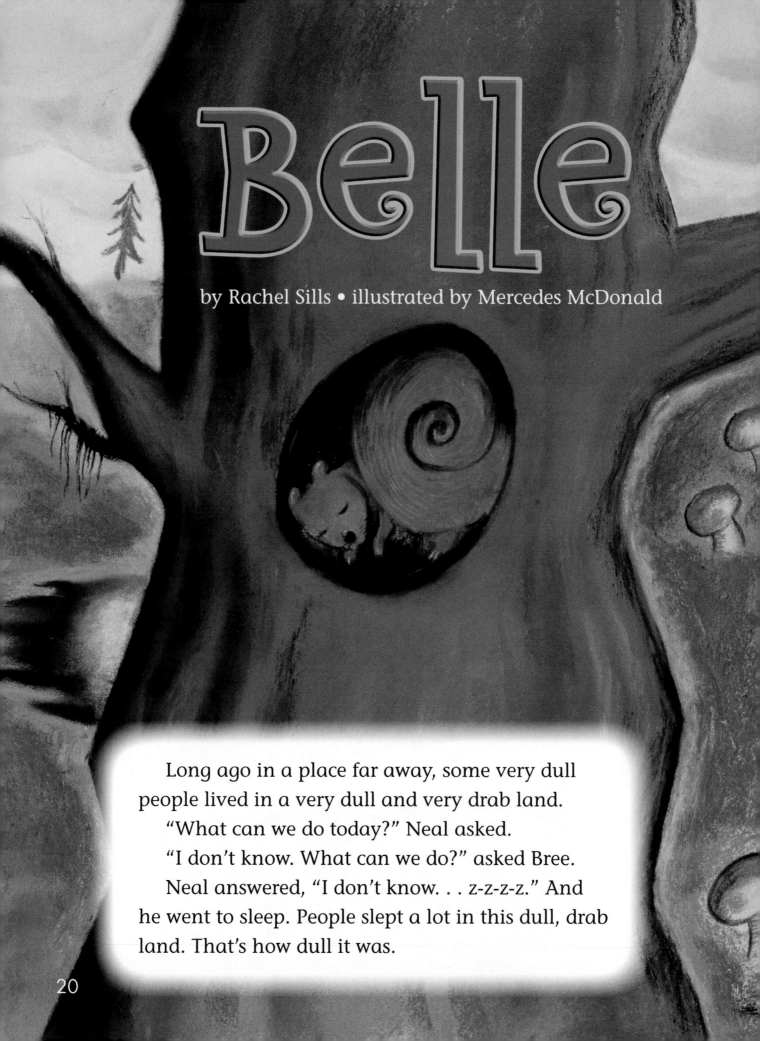

Belle

by Rachel Sills • illustrated by Mercedes McDonald

Long ago in a place far away, some very dull people lived in a very dull and very drab land.

"What can we do today?" Neal asked.

"I don't know. What can we do?" asked Bree.

Neal answered, "I don't know. . . z-z-z-z." And he went to sleep. People slept a lot in this dull, drab land. That's how dull it was.

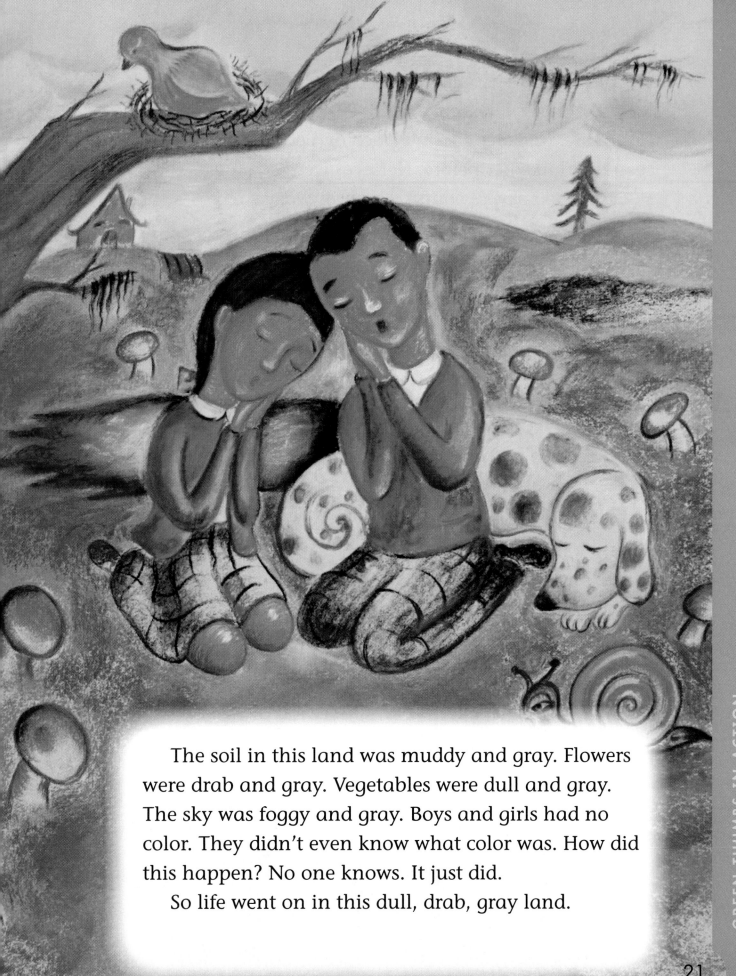

The soil in this land was muddy and gray. Flowers were drab and gray. Vegetables were dull and gray. The sky was foggy and gray. Boys and girls had no color. They didn't even know what color was. How did this happen? No one knows. It just did.

So life went on in this dull, drab, gray land.

One day, the people spotted a new girl. This girl didn't look like them. She didn't act like them. In fact, she had lots of life, and she had lots of color. People hadn't ever seen a girl like her before. Her eyes were as blue as the sky. Not their sky, of course. Her hair was as red as a rose. Not their roses, of course.

People began calling her Belle, because all day long she sang about blue bells and pretty shells. As she sang, she skipped over dull, gray farms. She went up drab, gray hills. She hopped over muddy ditches. And she scattered tiny things. What were they? What did she scatter on the soil? No one knew.

People asked Belle where she came from. But she just smiled. They asked what she was scattering. But she just smiled even more. Then, one day she left, just as fast as she had come. And in a short time, those dull people forgot her.

A year passed. The land was still gray. Flowers were still drab. Vegetables were still dull. The sky was still foggy and gray.

24

But one day, a change came. Tiny green plants started growing in the soil. They sprang up on the farms. They popped up on the hills. They burst up in the ditches.

"What's happening? Nothing looks the same! The hills are covered with green! The farms have green carpets! Even the trees are turning green!" cried Neal and Bree.

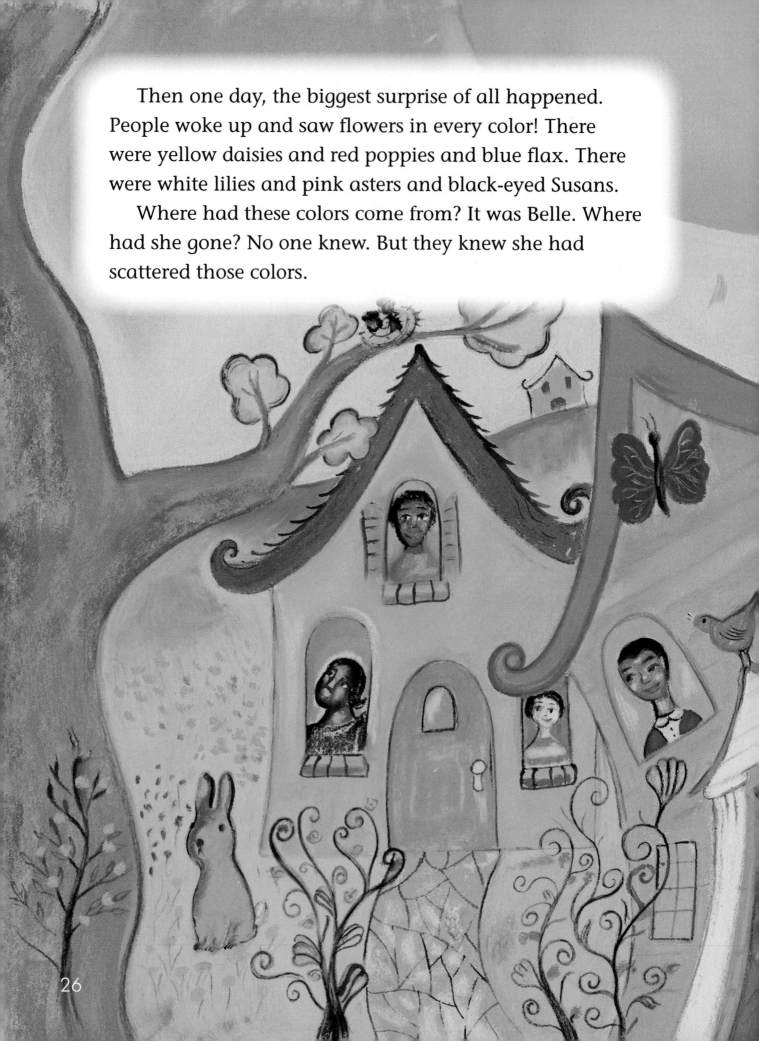

Then one day, the biggest surprise of all happened. People woke up and saw flowers in every color! There were yellow daisies and red poppies and blue flax. There were white lilies and pink asters and black-eyed Susans.

Where had these colors come from? It was Belle. Where had she gone? No one knew. But they knew she had scattered those colors.

That place began to change more and more. The sky turned blue, and the sun shone yellow. The land wasn't dull any more, so the people weren't dull. They smiled at each other and spoke of many things. They began growing more vegetables and even more flowers. And no one went to sleep in the day. There was too much to do. Now they had to scatter colors just as Belle had.

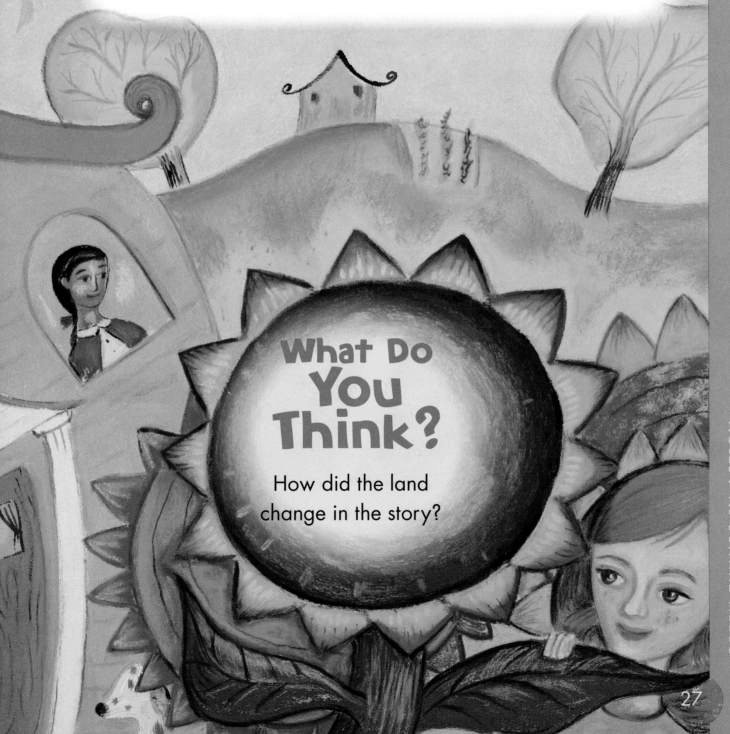

What Do You Think?

How did the land change in the story?

27

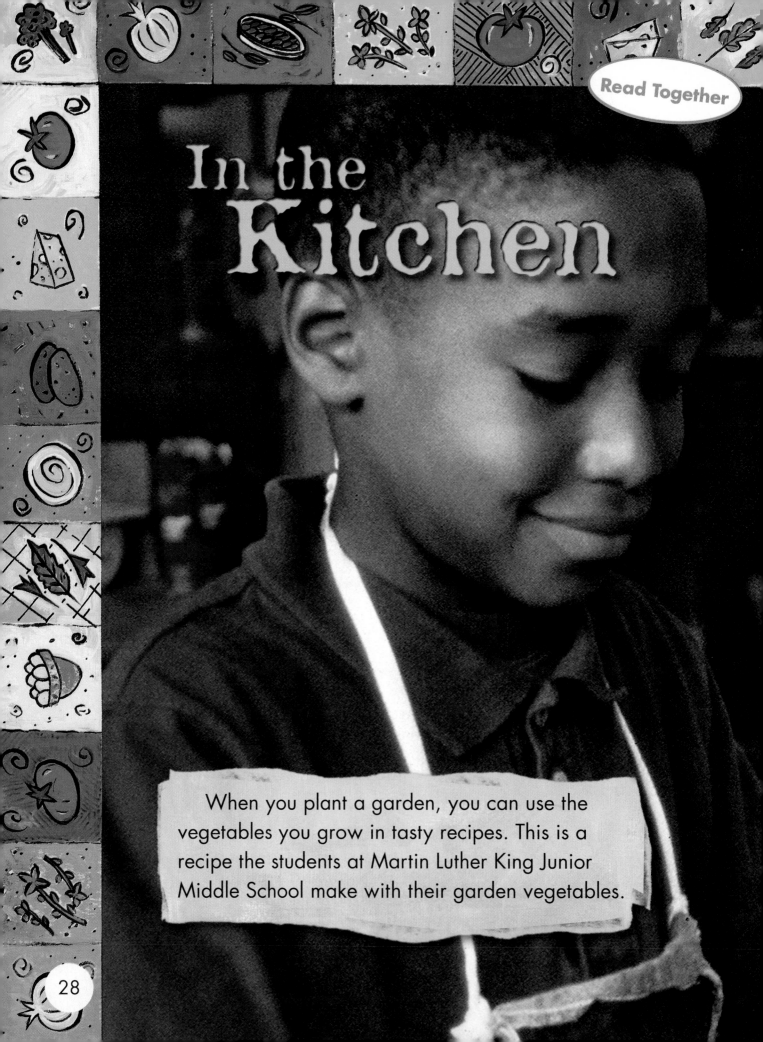

In the Kitchen

When you plant a garden, you can use the vegetables you grow in tasty recipes. This is a recipe the students at Martin Luther King Junior Middle School make with their garden vegetables.

Frittata

8 eggs, well beaten

2–3 cups assorted vegetables and herbs (any of these vegetables: chard, thyme, parsley, spinach, cooked potatoes, garlic, onion, tomato, basil, mushrooms—things you like!)

½ cup grated cheese

2 Tablespoons olive oil

Crack the eggs into a mixing bowl and beat well using a whisk. Wash and chop all vegetables and herbs. Heat olive oil in a skillet. Add the chopped herbs and vegetables and cook until slightly tender. Add the eggs and cheese, stirring well. Cook till eggs are halfway cooked. Finish in a hot oven (400°F) till puffy and golden brown and eggs are set. Time to eat!!!

4YOU2DO

Word Play

Can you name more flowers or vegetables? Make a list of each to find out.

Making Connections

People in Babylon planted gardens in the desert. Aztec people planted crops in marshes. Belle planted pretty plants in a drab, dull land. How did each of them make the land better?

On Paper

You read about many different gardens. Which one would you most like to visit? Write about it. Tell what you think is special about it.

Possible answers to Word Play: Flowers—violet, buttercup, mum, rose, tulip; Vegetables—beets, carrots, lettuce, peas, onions

Contents

Words 2 the Wise

Nature has some secrets to share. What can they be? As you read, find out about **Nature: The True Story.**

Let's Explore

Secrets of Nature

What is a rainbow? Why do seasons change? What makes thunder? In the past, people did not know. They made up tales called myths to explain things in nature. Since those days, scientists have discovered why these things happen.

What is a rainbow?

Myth Long ago, a Greek myth tried to explain rainbows. Iris was the Greek goddess of rainbows. Iris used a rainbow as a road. Her rainbow went between her home in the sky and Earth.

Fact Scientists know that real rainbows form when sun shines on water droplets in the air. Water bends the sun's rays. That makes them split into colors.

Why do seasons change?

Myth Demeter (di-MEE-ter) was the Greek goddess of plants. She had a child who was kidnapped. Crops stopped growing because she was so sad. This was winter. When her child came back, Demeter let spring return.

Fact The Earth is tilted. When places on Earth are tilted toward the sun, it is summer. When places on Earth are tilted away from the sun, it is winter.

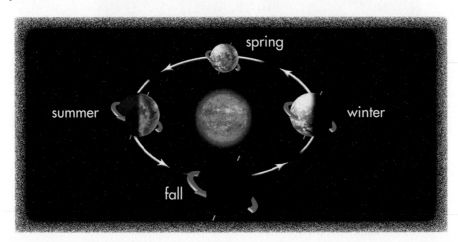

What makes thunder?

Myth In a Norse* myth, Thor was the god of thunder. Thor rode across the sky in a cart pulled by goats. When Thor tossed his huge hammer, it flashed and made thunder.

*__Norse__ Norse myths came from Scandinavia long ago. Sweden, Norway, and Denmark are in Scandinavia.

Fact Scientists know how storms with thunder form. At times, cold air clashes with warm, wet air. When that happens, it makes storms and thunder.

Explaining Nature's Secrets

by Paul Lynk

We've all seen nature at work. Plants and animals grow and change. Let's see how scientists explain some secrets of nature to us.

Me and My Shadow

Is your shadow long or short? You've seen it both ways. How can that be? Scientists get the answer from the sun. Shadows form when something blocks the sun's rays.

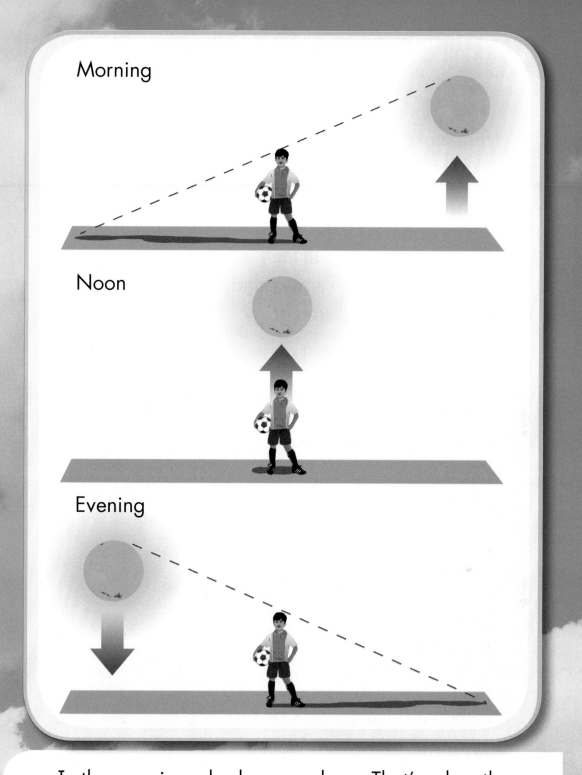

Morning

Noon

Evening

In the morning, shadows are long. That's when the sun is just rising. It is still low in the sky.

At lunch time, shadows are short. The sun shines straight down on us.

Late in the day, shadows are long again. The sun is setting. It is low in the sky again.

The Job of a Leaf

What makes a green leaf turn red or yellow? If we ask a scientist, we'd get this answer.

A green leaf has a big job. It helps feed the tree on which it grows. A leaf has green, red, and yellow pigments* inside it. In summer, green pigment works hard. It collects the sun's rays and uses them to feed the tree. This helps the tree grow.

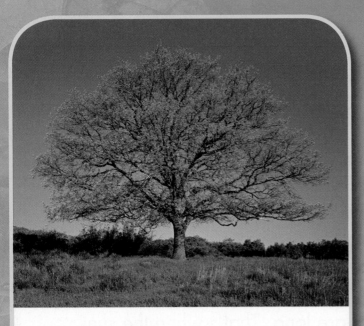

Spring Leaves bud out. The tree begins growing again.

Summer Green pigment collects the sun's rays. The tree grows.

*__pigment__ the part of a living thing that gives it its color

In winter, the tree needs to rest. It doesn't need to grow for a while. So it doesn't need to be fed. The green pigment fades. The yellow and red pigments take over. Then nature gives us a show of color just before winter starts.

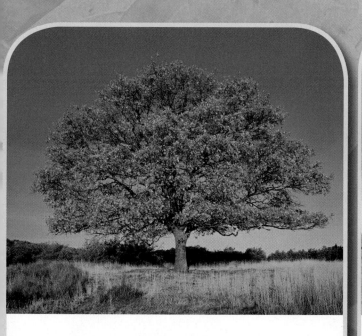

Fall The tree gets ready to rest. Red and yellow pigments take over.

Winter The tree rests during winter.

Secrets in a Tree Trunk

We know that trees grow each year, but a tree can't tell us its age. We can discover a tree's age only after it's been cut down. Scientists use growth rings in a tree trunk to discover a tree's age.

Look at a tree stump, and you'll see growth rings. Each ring stands for one year of growing. How many rings are there? That's the tree's age.

tree rings

Tree rings can also tell us about the climate in the past. A thick tree ring means the tree had plenty of rain and sun that year. A thin tree ring means that weather was bad or that insects or fire harmed the tree.

tree rings

Music Class for Birds

Did you know that birds must learn to sing? Scientists say baby birds first listen to grown-up birds. They try to sing what they hear. At first, their singing is more like screeching. That's because they're still learning. But they keep trying! Some scientists think baby birds dream about singing. Their dreams may help them learn their songs.

More Work to Do

Nature has lots more secrets. Scientists keep discovering them. They're trying to explain our world to us with facts. These days we don't need myths to understand nature. We can find out nature's secrets from scientists.

What Do You Think?

What are some secrets of nature that scientists have explained to us?

Scientists at Work

by Lindy Russell

You've read about things in nature that scientists can explain to us. Scientists have many different jobs. Let's take a look at some of them.

Scientists Who Study Plants

Some scientists study plants that we eat. They try to make plants that grow better. Their goal is to produce plenty of good crops to feed us well.

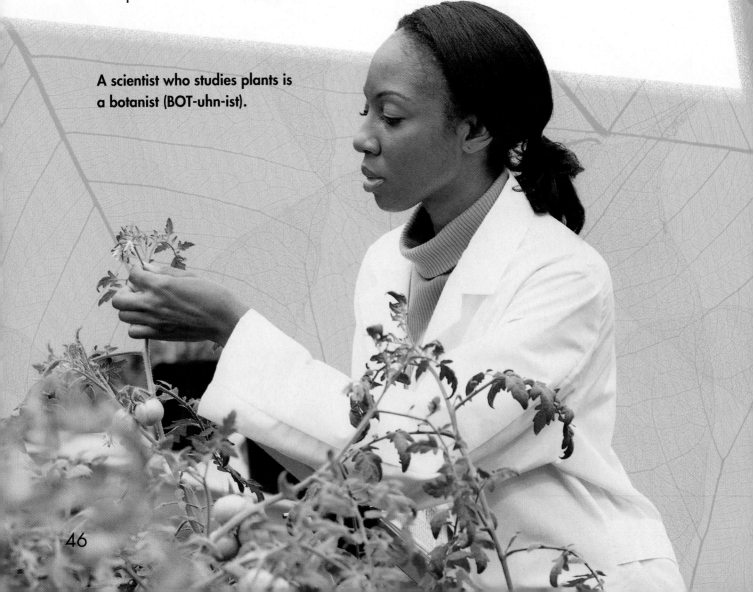

A scientist who studies plants is a botanist (BOT-uhn-ist).

Some scientists study plants to find cures for sick people. Many plants can help the sick. These scientists find out which plants can save lives.

Heart medicine comes from foxglove plants.

Scientists Who Study Animals

If you'd like to study animals, these jobs are for you. From tiny bugs to huge whales, there are plenty of animals to study.

Some scientists study insects, such as bees, that help us. These insects make things we use. Scientists who study these insects focus* on getting them to produce more of what we use.

*focus to pay close attention to something

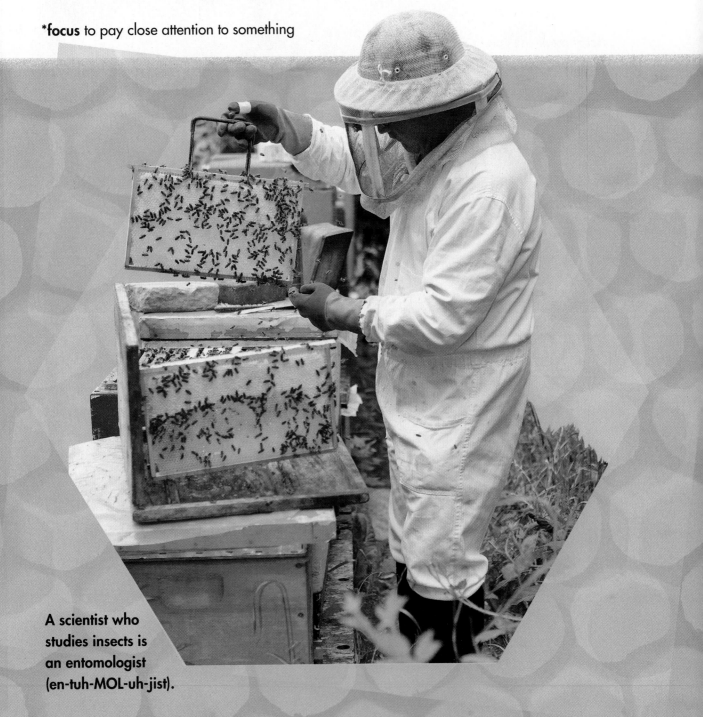

A scientist who studies insects is an entomologist (en-tuh-MOL-uh-jist).

Other insects can harm us and make us sick. Insects can eat crops and kill plants. Scientists study ways to prevent these problems.

If you'd like working with bigger animals, you may like being a vet. Some vets help pets. Other vets treat farm animals or wild animals. Vets help keep animals in good shape. Vets help sick or injured animals get better.

A doctor who treats animals is a veterinarian (vet-er-uh-NAIR-ee-uhn).

Scientists Who Study Fossils

Some scientists study the history of life on Earth. These scientists study fossils of plants and animals. Fossils are remains or marks left by living things from long ago.

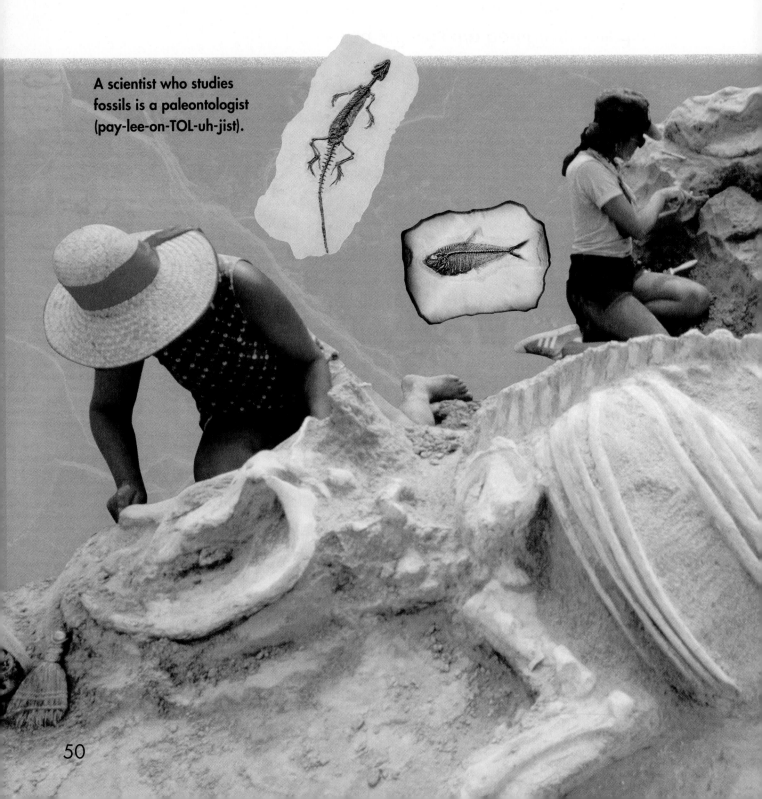

A scientist who studies fossils is a paleontologist (pay-lee-on-TOL-uh-jist).

A fossil can be a bone, or it can be the shape that an animal or plant left in a rock. Scientists who study fossils have discovered extinct animals, such as T. Rex, that aren't living now. Plant fossils help scientists discover what the climate was like on Earth long ago. These facts can help predict what may happen to our climate.

Scientists Who Study Weather

What will the weather be this week? Hot and sunny? Wet and rainy? Cold and snowy? Some scientists forecast* the weather.

People depend on weather forecasts. We use them to plan events such as picnics. Pilots use them to decide if it is safe to fly. Farmers use them to know if they must protect their crops from frost.

*__forecast__ to tell what is going to happen

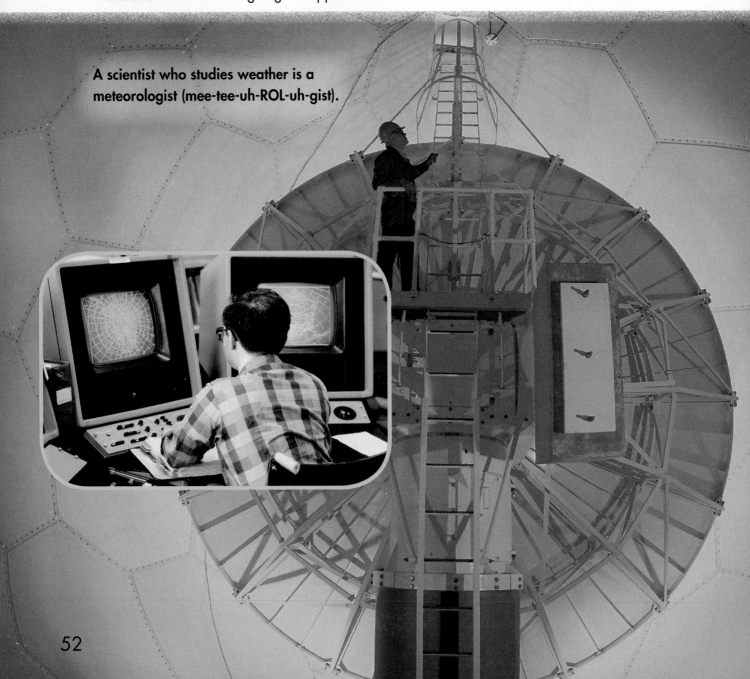

A scientist who studies weather is a meteorologist (mee-tee-uh-ROL-uh-gist).

Scientists who forecast weather use modern tools. Radar* detects, or spots, storms, strong winds, or other bad weather. Warning people about bad storms, such as tornadoes (tor-NAY-dohz), can save lives. People can take shelter or get out of the storm's path.

These scientists do important jobs. We're so glad that we can depend on them to tell us how nature works.

*radar a tool that uses radio waves to find unseen objects

What Do You Think?
Scientists have many different jobs. Tell why their jobs are important.

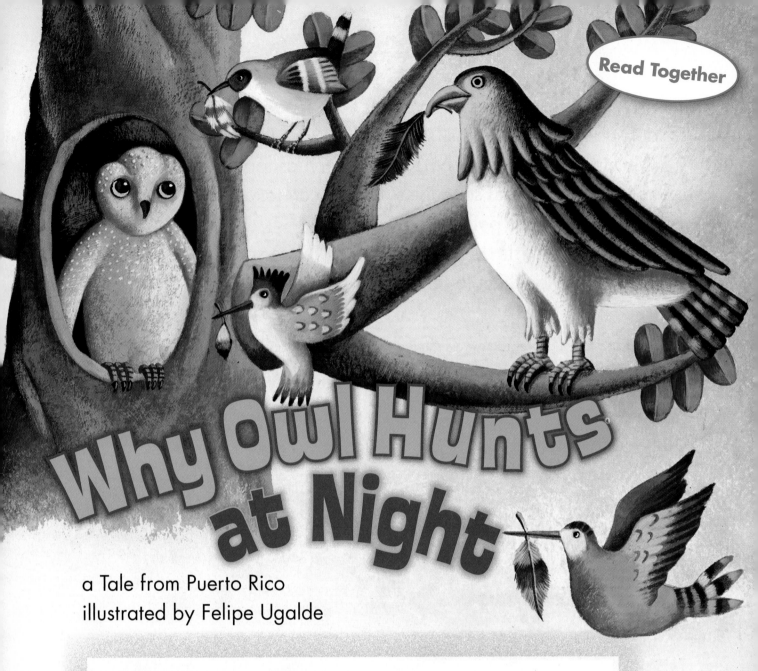

Why Owl Hunts at Night

a Tale from Puerto Rico
illustrated by Felipe Ugalde

Everyone knows that owls hunt only at night. But long ago owls hunted only by day! They had no feathers, so they needed the sun to keep them warm.

One night the birds decided to have a big party. But Owl said, "I can't go out at night. It's chilly, and I've no feathers to keep me warm."

Eagle said, "You're right. I have an idea! We can each loan you a feather. Then you'd be warm."

All the birds loaned Owl some feathers. "You must return them tomorrow," Eagle told Owl.

Owl looked beautiful in his friends' feathers! He had a wonderful time at the party. And, for a change, he felt warm. As it grew late, Owl thought about returning the feathers. But he didn't want to be cold and plain ever again. Just before the party ended, Owl flew away.

The next day all the birds tried to find Owl. They're still looking to this very day. And that is why Owl comes out only at night. He knows that other birds sleep at night. And he doesn't want to give back his warm, beautiful feathers.

4 You 2 Do

Word Play

How much do you know about scientists? Make a word web for the word **scientist** to find out. Can you include all these words in your web?

discover   environment   problem

weather   nature   solution

scientist

Making Connections

Which kind of scientist studies thunder? tree rings? why leaves change color? how birds learn to sing?

On Paper

If you were a scientist, what would you want to study in nature? Write about it and tell why it interests you.

A CLOSER LOOK

Contents

Words 2 the Wise

We can use our senses to learn more about nature. As you read, think about what nature can teach us when we take **a closer look.**

Using Our Senses

Our five senses are sight, smell, hearing, touch, and taste. We can use our five senses to help us learn about nature.

You're in school now. But let's pretend we're on a forest trail. What will we discover when we use our senses?

Sight In a forest we will see trees, right? What kind do you think we'll see? Is sunshine shining on their branches? Will we spot a butterfly or a toad? Maybe we'll see a deer.

Smell Let's take a big whiff. What can we smell? Can we smell wildflowers that grow here? Pine trees? A skunk? How would that smell?

Hearing Stop and listen. What can we hear? Is a bluebird chirping nearby? Are insects buzzing? Perhaps a classmate is speaking. Shhh, let's listen to the forest.

Touch Now you've picked up a pinecone. Do you like how it feels? Let's touch some moss* on a tree. Is it soft or scratchy?

62 ***moss** small green plants that grow close together

Taste Perhaps this forest has an apple tree. Shall we taste an apple? No, we'd better let the birds eat them.

We're using our senses every moment of every day. Use your senses on your trip home today. What will you see, smell, hear, touch, or taste?

A Lesson from Mother Nature

by Phyllis Perry

Scientists use their senses of taste, touch, hearing, sight, and smell. They need them to observe nature. Nature might help them get some grand ideas.

Leonardo da Vinci (lee-uh-NARD-oh duh VIN-chee)

The great artist Leonardo da Vinci lived long ago. This man was a scientist as well as an artist. He spent days observing birds in flight. This sight made him wonder how a bird flies.

Leonardo sketched birds taking off and landing. Birds use wings to fly. How do birds' wings work? Could men fly with wings too? Leonardo sketched his ideas for flying machines. Leonardo never made a flying machine that worked. But later his ideas helped people build airplanes and gliders.*

*gliders light airplanes with no engines

Sir Isaac Newton (EYE-zuhk NOOT-n)

Have you ever gotten big ideas while resting? That's what happened to Sir Isaac Newton. About 300 years ago, he had a taste for an apple. While he sat outside by an apple tree, an apple fell next to him. This sight made him start to think. Why did that apple go down and not up or to the side?

Isaac decided a special force must be pulling the apple to earth. He named that pulling force *gravity*. Gravity doesn't work just on apples. People are held on Earth by this force too. In fact, gravity works on everything. The bigger something is, the more gravity pulls on it.

Joseph Glidden

About 150 years ago, many families in the United States moved west. Some became ranchers. Ranchers needed a way to keep their ranch animals in one place. Other people in the West had farms. How could ranchers make sure their animals didn't touch farm crops?

Joseph Glidden observed that animals didn't like touching plants and shrubs that had thorns. Could this idea help keep animals in one place? Joseph tried adding sharp bits of metal, or barbs, to wire. The wire felt like it had thorns. Joseph tied this barbed wire around animal pens. It worked! It kept animals penned inside.

Ellen Ochoa (oh-CHOH-uh)

We use our sense of sight to understand things around us. When we look at something, our eyes tell us about it. Is it the same as other things we see? Or is it different?

Ellen Ochoa invented a machine that works like our eyes. This machine can look at things and tell if they are the same or different. It can spot mistakes as products are being made. Then the mistakes can be fixed.

Three years after Ochoa invented this machine, NASA chose her as an astronaut.

What can Mother Nature show you? Think about what you see, hear, taste, touch, or smell. Can you get an idea from nature? You might think up the next big invention!

What Do You Think?

How can observing things in nature help scientists get ideas?

Tracking a Storm

by Cody McCalister
illustrated by Karen Lee

Hector and Clint lived across the road from each other for many years. But last summer Clint's dad switched jobs, and his family moved to Texas. The boys stay in touch with e-mail.

File Edit View Favorites Tools Help

To: Clint
Subject: Storm

Clint,

I just watched a news report with Mom and Dad. It showed that a big storm might hit the Texas coast. It said the storm is growing. What's the weather like near you?

My teacher this year is Mister Bennett. How's your new school?

Hector

To: Hector
Subject: re: Storm

Hector,

The storm might hit tomorrow afternoon. I can feel the wind picking up, and I can taste sea air. Soon we're going inland. We'll stay with family friends.

My dog Flash will stay with our neighbor Mister Dean. Mister Dean is staying home during the storm. He's seen storms like this before.

This weekend should be something!

Clint

To: Clint
Subject: re: Storm

Clint,

I don't know when you'll read this, but I just had to write. It looks like the storm just came on shore about 50 miles north of your city. I hope everyone is OK.

Hector

To: Hector
Subject: re: Storm

Hector,
    I'm online at the place where we're staying. We've been watching TV all day too. It looks pretty bad where the storm hit. Dad thinks our home might be OK, but we haven't been able to get in touch with Mister Dean. I'm worried about Flash. Flash hates storms.

Clint

To: Clint
Subject: re: Storm

Clint,
   The news reports have shown some people returning home. Are you home yet?

Hector

To: Hector
Subject: re: Storm

Hector,

We're home. There are branches scattered in our backyard, and a funny smell is coming up from our basement. Water got in during the storm. It sure feels hot in here.

Mister Dean said Flash ran away right after the storm. But he came back. He sure was a sight for sore eyes!

Clint

What Do You Think?

Why did Clint's family go inland before the storm hit?

How to Be a

Observing birds can be fun. Here are some things you might do.

• Go someplace that birds like. This might be a park, a pond, or even your backyard.

• Use binoculars if you have them. They will give you a closer look at the birds.

• Use a bird book to help you name each bird.

• Keep a list of all the birds you see.

Bird Watcher

Here are two hints to remember.

- If you start feeding birds, keep it up. The birds will depend on you.

- When you watch birds, don't ever disturb their nests.

Invite a Bird to Lunch

- Find a pinecone.
- Tie a string around the wide end.
- Spread peanut butter over the cone.
- Roll it in birdseeds.
- Hang the pinecone from a tree.
- Watch the birds get a closer look!

4 YOU 2 DO

Word Play

Make compound words using these words.

some	every	sun	thing	side
work	shine	light	in	home
one	out	body	land	house

Making Connections

Scientists get ideas for inventions from nature. Now it's your turn to make up an invention. Use an idea from nature. Draw a picture of your invention and write about it.

On Paper

Think of a place you like and pretend you're there. Then write what you would see, hear, smell, feel, and taste while visiting there. Can anyone guess the place you wrote about?

Possible answers for Word Play: someone, somebody, something, everyone, everybody, everything, sunshine, sunlight, inside, inland, outside, workout, homework, homeland, lighthouse, housework

TO THE RESCUE!

Contents

TO THE RESCUE!

Let's Explore

What comes to mind when you see the words
extinct and *endangered*?

Some animals struggle to survive. As you read, look for ways that people come **to the rescue.**

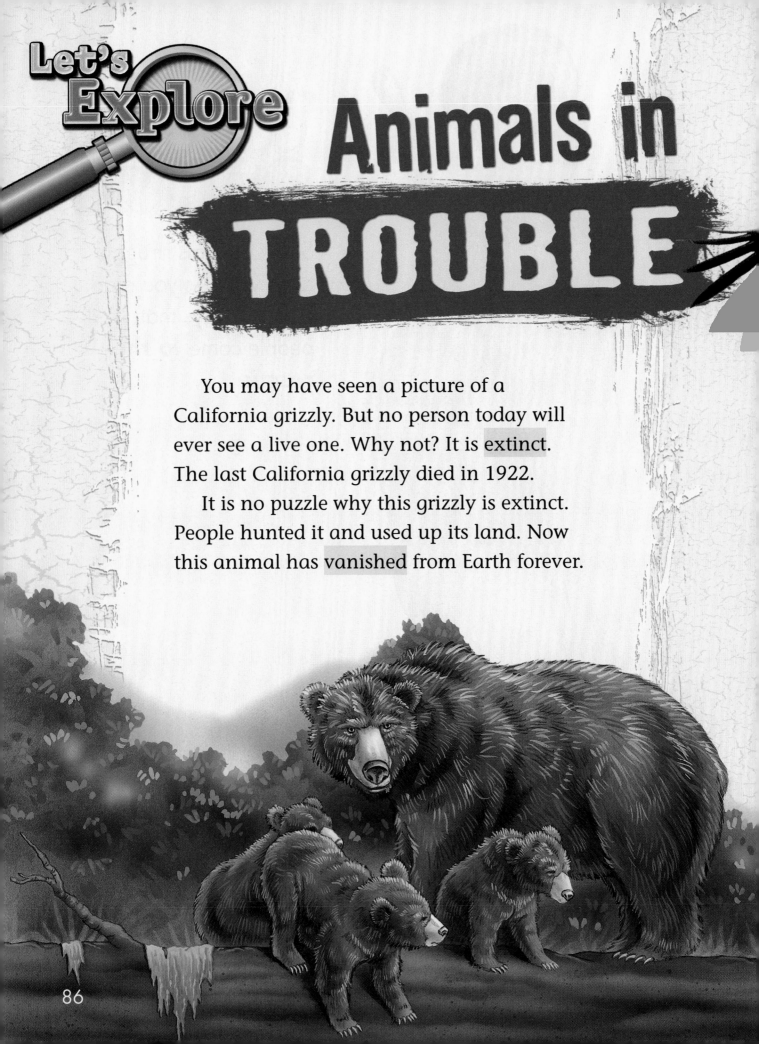

Let's Explore

Animals in TROUBLE

You may have seen a picture of a California grizzly. But no person today will ever see a live one. Why not? It is extinct. The last California grizzly died in 1922.

It is no puzzle why this grizzly is extinct. People hunted it and used up its land. Now this animal has vanished from Earth forever.

A condor soars through the air above the Sierra Madre Mountains in California.

The California condor is endangered. That means that few condors are living today. Many of these big birds used to live in the wild. But then people settled near condors' homes. The condors had no place to nest and bring up their young. Also, condors often ate parts of animals killed by hunters. Gunshot left in those animals made the condors get sick and die.

Dark California condors with numbered tags

By the 1980s, condors had almost vanished. The outlook for them was grim.* But then animal experts tackled the problem. They made a plan to rescue the condors. They decided to trap the wild condors and bring them to a safe place. If the condors could survive in this safe place, their numbers might grow. Then some condors could return to the wild.

*grim not hopeful

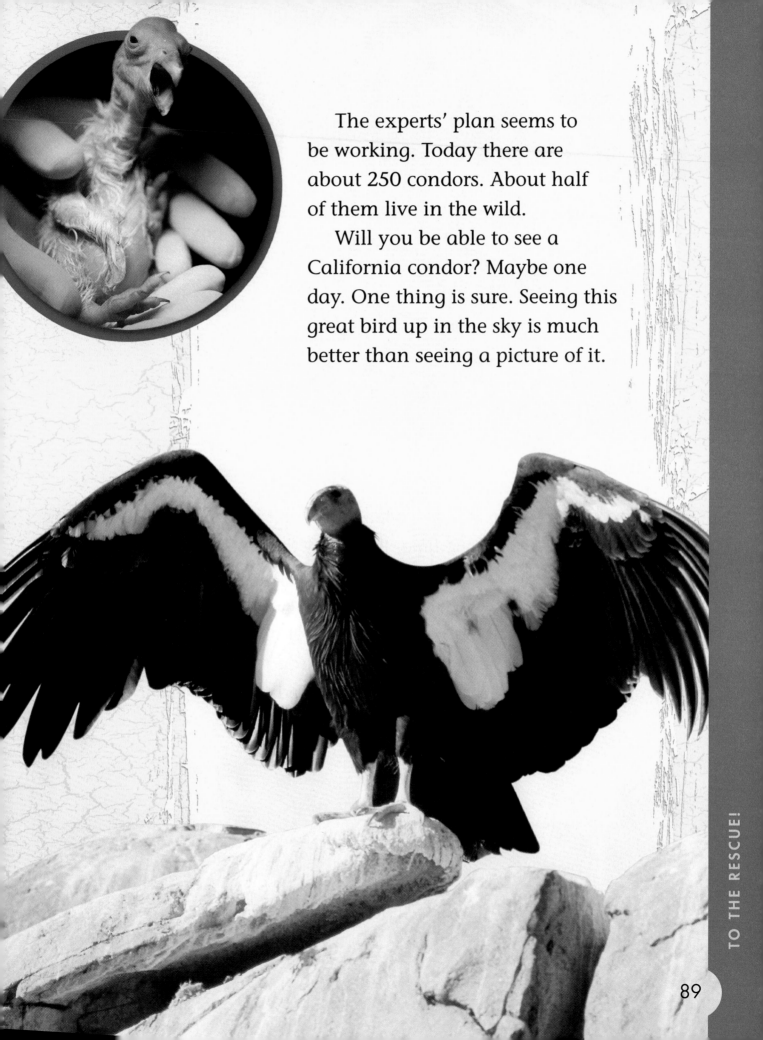

The experts' plan seems to be working. Today there are about 250 condors. About half of them live in the wild.

Will you be able to see a California condor? Maybe one day. One thing is sure. Seeing this great bird up in the sky is much better than seeing a picture of it.

Rules to Protect

by Julie Lavender

This bundle of fur is a sea otter pup. Don't you just want to cuddle it? At one time, this perky little creature was almost extinct. Back in the 1700s, people hunted sea otters for their furry skins, or pelts. These pelts were soft and beautiful. They would sell for a lot of money. But in their rush to get rich, people killed far too many sea otters. In time, most sea otters had vanished.

Animals

In 1911, some countries decided to protect endangered sea otters. Leaders of these lands met and discussed how to handle the problem. First, they agreed on a set of rules. Then they signed a treaty,* the Fur Seal Treaty. This treaty said that people could not hunt sea otters. Thanks to this treaty, sea otters are not extinct today.

*__treaty__ a promise countries make to one another that says what they will or will not do

Today many countries try to protect endangered animals and plants. In fact, 169 countries signed a treaty called CITES (SYT-eez). This treaty has rules that limit trade, or buying and selling, in endangered live animals and plants. This treaty also limits trade in plants and animal parts and in things made from plants and animals.

Police in Thailand find elephant tusks at an airport. Someone was trying to smuggle, or sneak, them out of the country.

The elephant is an animal that CITES is helping. Countries that belong to CITES will not let people buy or sell elephant tusks. By stopping this trade, it is hoped that fewer elephants will be killed for their tusks. Then more elephants will survive.

Elephants at Risk

- The number of elephants in Africa is shrinking. There are just 400,000 to 600,000 elephants in Africa today. That is less than half as many as in 1979.

- People are the main reason elephants are in danger. Hunters kill elephants for their tusks. People settle on their land and drive them away.

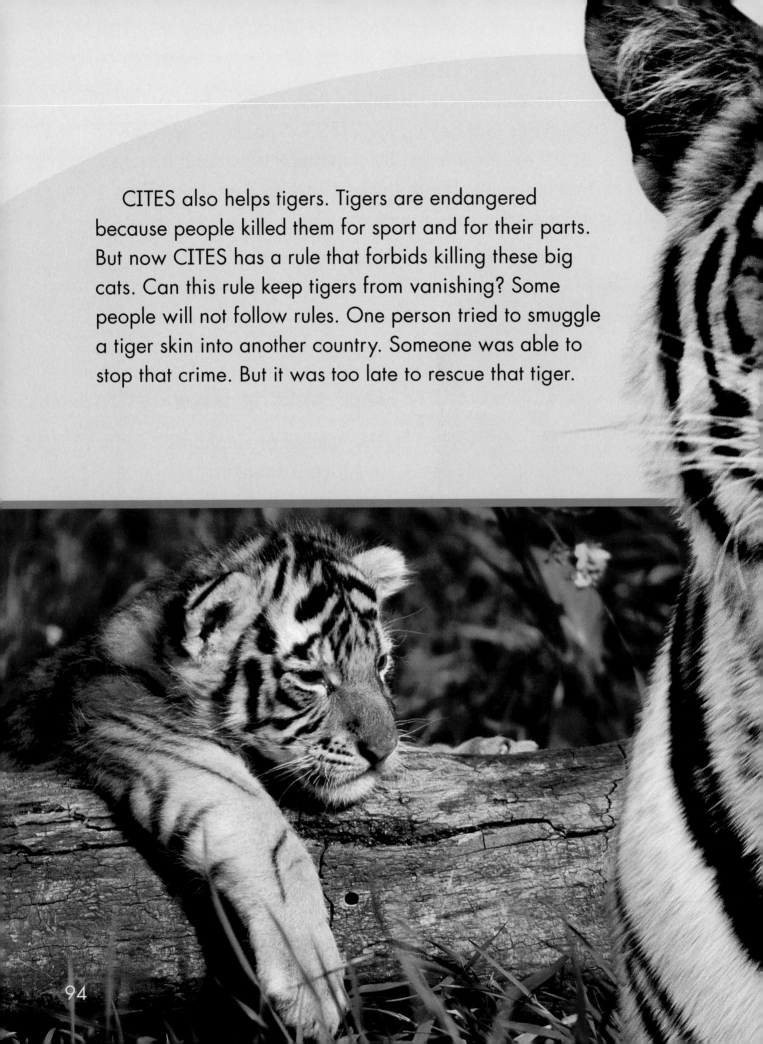

CITES also helps tigers. Tigers are endangered because people killed them for sport and for their parts. But now CITES has a rule that forbids killing these big cats. Can this rule keep tigers from vanishing? Some people will not follow rules. One person tried to smuggle a tiger skin into another country. Someone was able to stop that crime. But it was too late to rescue that tiger.

Tigers in Trouble

- In 1900, more than 100,000 tigers lived in the wild. Today just about 7,000 tigers are left.
- People still hunt tigers for their parts, even though a rule forbids it.
- People cut down forests where tigers live. When tigers cannot find enough to eat, they may attack people or farm animals. Then people kill them.
- People settle on tigers' land. This splits up tiger families. Tiger cubs are not able to survive.

Remember that furry sea otter pup? It is not extinct because people made rules to protect it. Rules are helping rescue elephants and tigers too. But many animals are still at risk.

Can you do anything to help rescue them? One simple step is to write a letter. You can write to a leader in the country where the endangered animal lives. Tell why that animal must be protected. Then one day CITES members may pass a rule to protect that animal. Perhaps one more animal will not vanish from Earth.

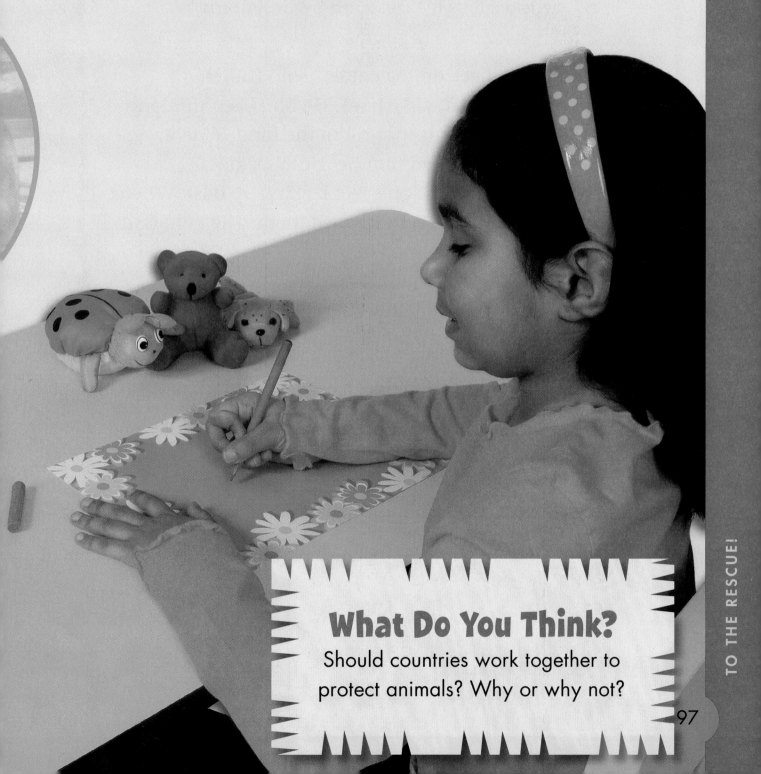

What Do You Think?

Should countries work together to protect animals? Why or why not?

Kisham and the Elephants

by Jelani Brown • illustrated by Gary Torrisi

"Kisham, go check on the cattle," said Father.

Father's words startled Kisham. He had been thinking about the wild elephants that roam the land. Where were they now? How he wished that he could see one.

Kisham ran up the hill, his feet kicking up dust. Where were Father's cattle? Then he spotted them. The herd had moved to find more grass to eat.

The herd was safe, but all around the grass was thin. The cattle did not have much grass to eat.

Just then Kisham heard a high burst, like a bugle. It seemed to come from nearby.

"Elephants!" he cried. Kisham turned and ran down the hill. Maybe he would get his wish. Maybe he would see an elephant today.

Kisham ran to his father, who seemed upset.

"Go away! Get off my land!" Father yelled at the elephants that trampled his grass. He waved his stick.

"But they are so grand, Father," Kisham gasped.

"Yes, elephants are grand," Father replied. "But if they trample the little bit of grass that is left on my land, my cattle will not be able to eat."

That night Kisham dreamed of elephants padding through thick green grass.

The next morning, as Kisham dressed, he heard a distant blast. Then he heard it again. "Gunfire," Kisham whispered to himself. He raced outside.

"Father!" Kisham called. "Come quick! I think the elephants may be in danger!"

Kisham and his father followed the dusty elephant tracks. They found the spot where the elephants had stopped to take a mud bath. They passed a little tree the elephants had toppled over. Then they found it.

The huge beast lay on its side in the dirt, as still as a rock. Flies buzzed around its head and tail. There were two white stumps where its two tusks had been.

"No!" Kisham cried.

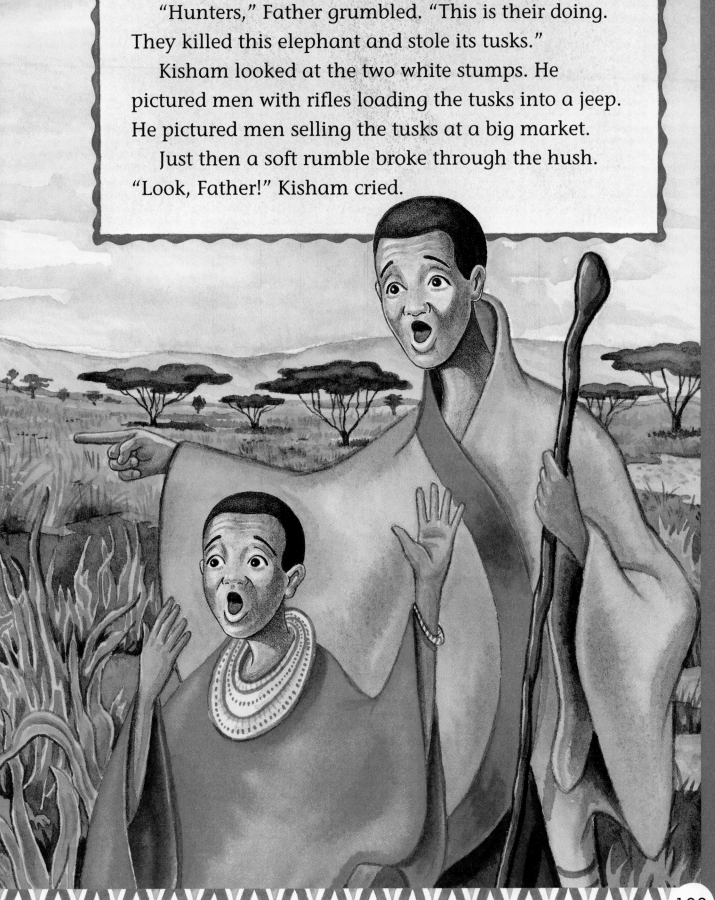

"Hunters," Father grumbled. "This is their doing. They killed this elephant and stole its tusks."

Kisham looked at the two white stumps. He pictured men with rifles loading the tusks into a jeep. He pictured men selling the tusks at a big market.

Just then a soft rumble broke through the hush. "Look, Father!" Kisham cried.

103

A baby elephant with big eyes and floppy ears was rubbing its trunk against the body in the dirt.

"A baby elephant!" Kisham cried. "We must rescue it, Father. It will not survive by itself."

Father patted Kisham on the back. "Yes, we must help," he said. "We will keep following the tracks in the dust. Perhaps they will lead us to this little one's family."

They traveled for miles. At last they found the elephants standing in the shade of a big tree. This time Father did not yell or wave his stick at the huge beasts. This time he just watched the baby elephant go back to its herd.

What Do You Think?

Did Father feel the same as Kisham about the elephants? Tell how each one felt.

Gone...but Not Forgotten

Hundreds of animals are now extinct. These are some of them. No one knows which animal will be next.

Carolina Parakeet
Extinct: 1920

Quagga
Extinct: 1883

N

Steller's Sea Cow
Extinct: 1768

People take over land and cut down forests. Then animals have fewer places to live. People add waste to the air and water. That makes animals sick. People hunt animals. Then animals cannot grow up and produce new young. As animals become extinct, new animals are not taking their place.

Tasmanian Tiger
Extinct: 1930s

Giant Moa
Extinct: 1600s

Dodo
Extinct: 1681

4 You 2 Do

Word Play

Make a word web for *extinct* and another for *endangered*. Work with a partner. Add words and categories to the webs. How big can your word webs get? Which web is bigger?

Making Connections

Why did Kisham and his father and the members of CITES take steps to protect animals?

On Paper

Kisham and his father saved the baby elephant by returning it to its herd. Many countries have helped animals by making rules to protect them. What could people in your community do to help endangered animals?

Contents

Dodging Disasters

110

Words 2 the Wise

A flood is a natural disaster. So is a hurricane. What do you do in a disaster like these? Read to find out about **dodging disasters.**

Natural Disasters

EVACUATION ROUTE

What do a hurricane, flood, earthquake, and blizzard have in common? They're all natural disasters. A hurricane is a storm that starts over a sea. When it hits land, watch out! Lots of rain, howling winds, and huge waves crash on shore. Hurricane winds can be around one hundred miles an hour. A hurricane can wash away beaches and bring down trees.

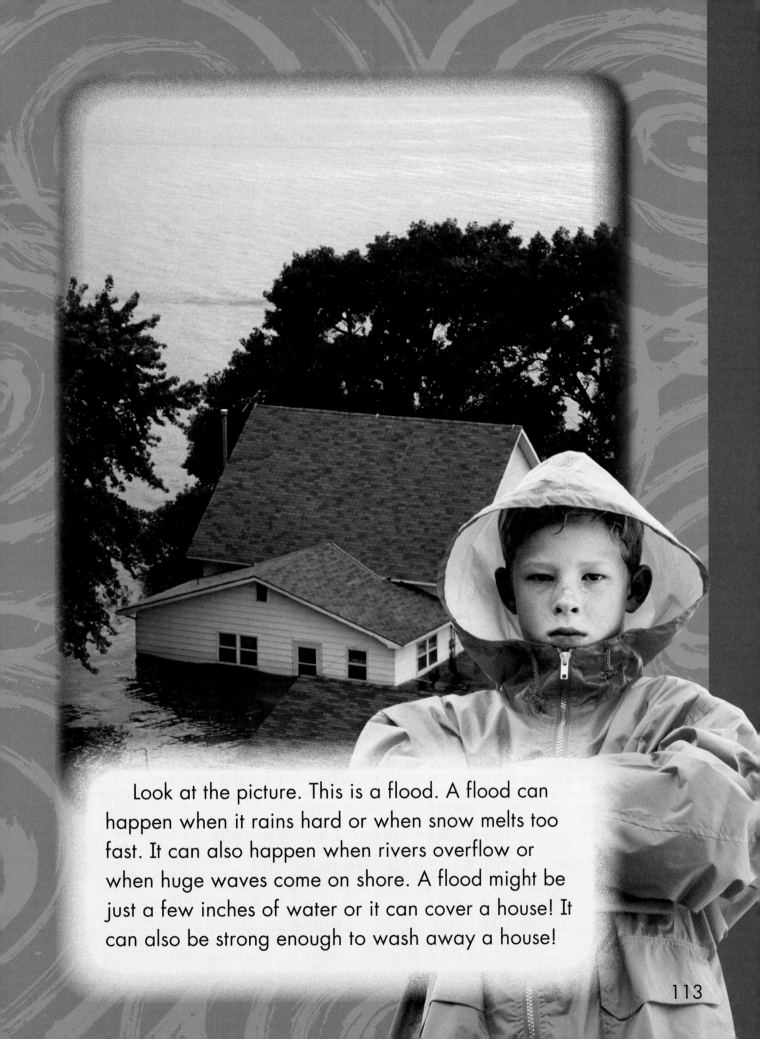

Look at the picture. This is a flood. A flood can happen when it rains hard or when snow melts too fast. It can also happen when rivers overflow or when huge waves come on shore. A flood might be just a few inches of water or it can cover a house! It can also be strong enough to wash away a house!

An earthquake happens when rock far below the ground breaks apart and shifts. This makes the ground shake. You might see things on a shelf wobble. You might hear a sound like thunder. One man said an earthquake felt like riding a bike down steps.

An earthquake can happen without any warning. Large earthquakes can wipe out houses and roads.

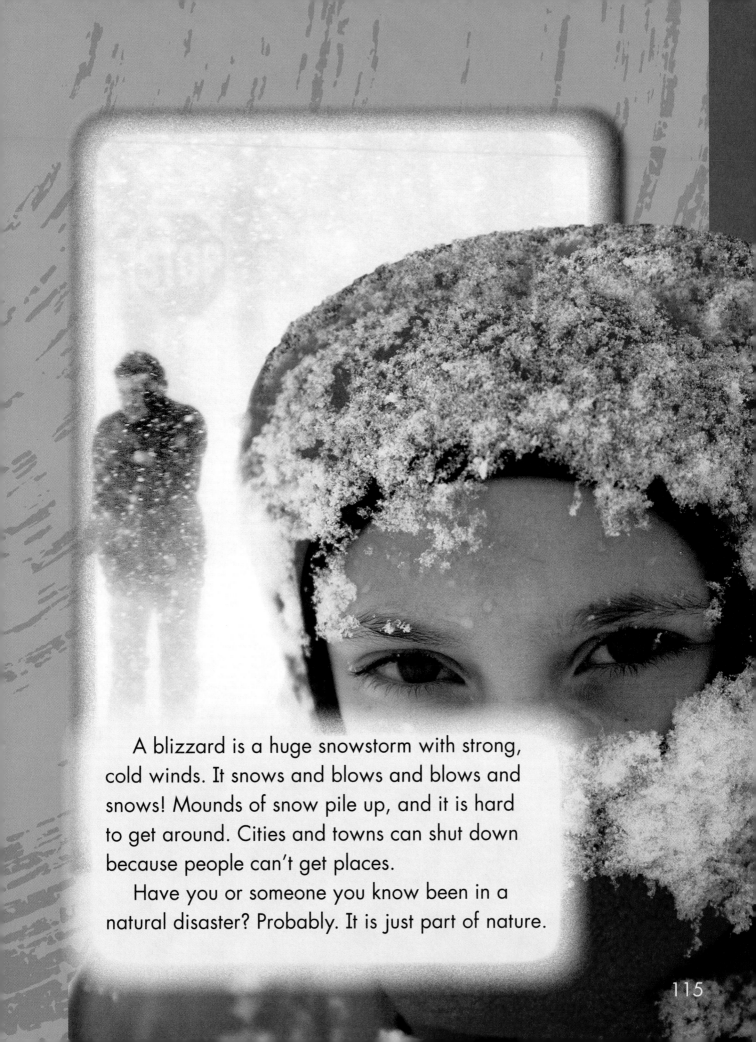

A blizzard is a huge snowstorm with strong, cold winds. It snows and blows and blows and snows! Mounds of snow pile up, and it is hard to get around. Cities and towns can shut down because people can't get places.

Have you or someone you know been in a natural disaster? Probably. It is just part of nature.

Tornadoes

by Ann Kovach

It's a hot summer day. A little dust swirls above the ground. Soon raindrops start to come down lightly. Plip! Plop! The sky darkens and the rain comes down harder and harder. Plip, plop, plop! Lightning flashes and hail* mixes in with the rain. Hailstones the size of apples pound the ground. And just as quick as the hail started, it stops.

*hail small, round pieces of ice that fall like rain

116

The air is still. But now, look up! There's a dark cloud hanging low in the sky. Suddenly a funnel of twisting wind comes down from that dark cloud. It hisses as it gets closer to the ground and touches the Earth. It spins and roars across the ground. What is happening? Quick, run for cover! It's a tornado!

A tornado is a powerful and forceful windstorm. Look at the picture. This is what a tornado looks like. Can you see the funnel cloud? Winds twist and spin inside it. Its winds can blow up to 300 miles an hour. That's really fast! It's about five times as fast as a car driving on a highway! Another name for a tornado is twister.

Of all storms a tornado is one of nature's worst. It can lift cars and turn them over. It can pick up animals as big as cows and carry them miles away. It can smash one house to bits yet not touch the one next to it. It can hurl trash everywhere. A twister can wreck anything in its path. And it can happen quickly without any warning.

119

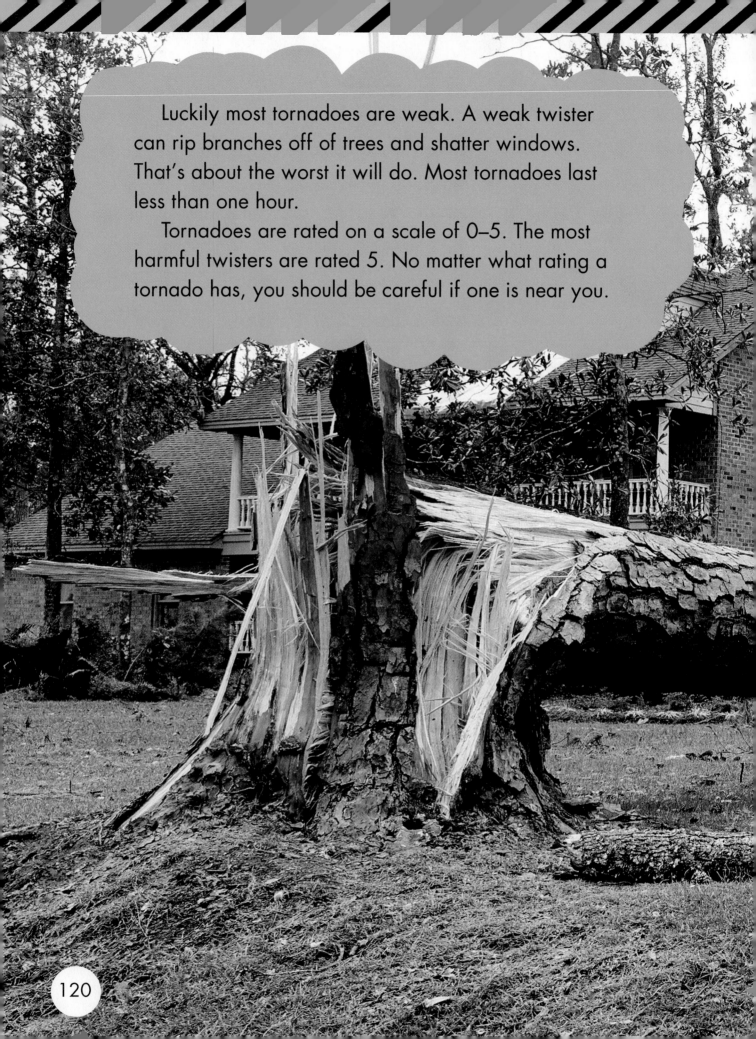

Luckily most tornadoes are weak. A weak twister can rip branches off of trees and shatter windows. That's about the worst it will do. Most tornadoes last less than one hour.

Tornadoes are rated on a scale of 0–5. The most harmful twisters are rated 5. No matter what rating a tornado has, you should be careful if one is near you.

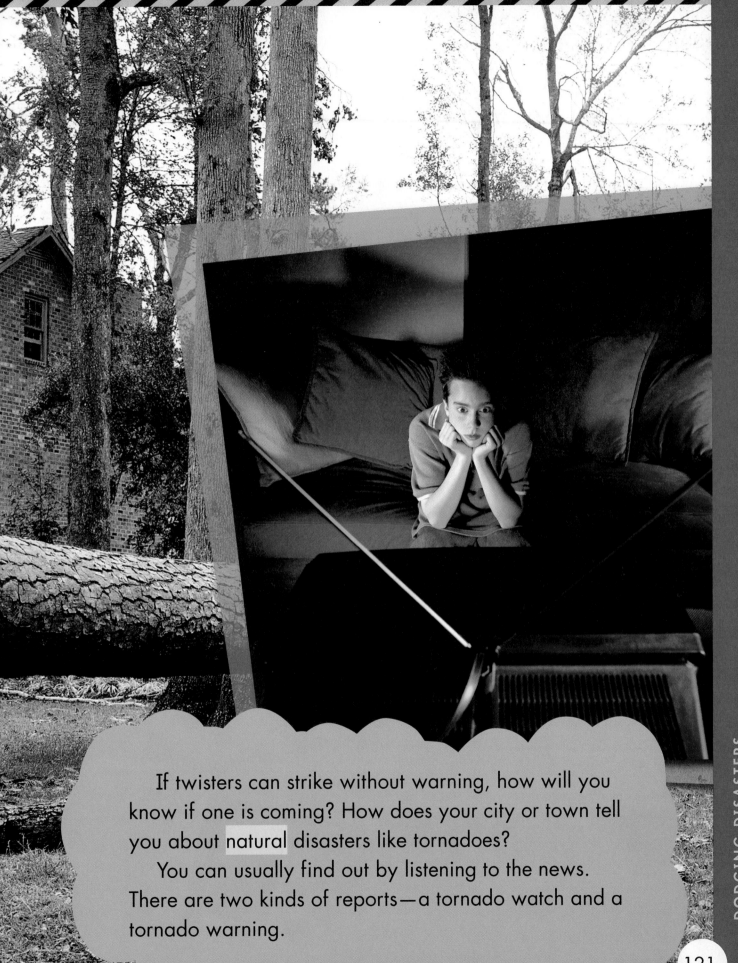

If twisters can strike without warning, how will you know if one is coming? How does your city or town tell you about natural disasters like tornadoes?

You can usually find out by listening to the news. There are two kinds of reports—a tornado watch and a tornado warning.

If you hear a tornado watch, listen for more facts. Observe the weather outside. A tornado watch tells you that a tornado might happen. But if you hear a tornado warning, find shelter quickly. A tornado warning means that a twister has been spotted!

Do you know what to do if you are in a tornado? Does your family and school have an emergency plan?

Here are some tornado tips. If you are inside, stay far away from windows. Go to the lowest place in the building. If you are outside, do not try to run. Lie down flat in a ditch or on low ground. Cover the back of your head with your arms.

If you are in a tornado, stay put until the danger has passed. It will.

What Do You Think?
What makes a tornado a natural disaster?

From Sun to Storm

by Gabriella Hale
illustrated by Amy Huntington

The Florida beach was nice. The sun shined brightly
and gentle waves bounced to shore. I liked collecting
shells and swimming in the warm sea.

"This is fun," I shouted from the water.

But in an instant, the fun would end.

A neighbor came running down the beach. "There's a
hurricane warning," he said, barely able to speak.

We quickly ran home. Mom turned on the radio.

"We interrupt this program for an emergency weather report," the speaker said. "This is a hurricane warning. Strong winds, heavy rains, and large floods are predicted. People on the coast are advised to move out."

We had to act fast. This was an emergency!

We knew what to do. We had made a hurricane plan long ago. I grabbed blankets and pillows. Mom got water and things to eat. Dad boarded up windows to protect them from the wind.

"Howard, don't forget the first aid kit," Mom shouted loudly.

We packed up the car. It was time to go inland.

I looked out the window as we drove away. It was drizzling lightly. Suddenly the sky got very dark. Clouds came from nowhere and surrounded us. Thunder growled loudly and lightning flashed. The rain came down more heavily and pounded the street. A powerful wind howled and pushed our car from side to side. Waves crashed on the beach.

"I'm scared," I said. "Will we be OK?"

"We'll be fine," Dad answered. "The weather is really bad here. But it will get better as we get farther away from the coast."

"We left in time," said Mom. "We're safe now. Luckily, we had a plan for an emergency. That's how we got out quickly."

Two hours later we reached a hotel in an inland town. A crowd was watching TV in the lobby.

A reporter was speaking. "Right now the waters are calm. That's because we are in the eye of the storm. But when the eye passes, powerful winds and rain will be back. This hurricane can last for hours.

"Many houses along the coast have been wrecked. Tree limbs have been broken. And as you can see, branches are scattered everywhere. You can also see the big flood in the street behind me. People are floating on make-shift rafts in efforts to survive," the reporter said.

"Will people get help?" I asked.

"Rescue teams will get there as soon as they can," Mom answered.

I was grateful we got out of the storm safely. But I felt bad for the people on TV. I hugged Mom and Dad tightly and hoped that the sun would come out shortly.

What Do You Think?
What was this family's plan? How did it help them survive the hurricane?

It's an Emergency!

Emergencies can happen without any warning. It is always best to prepare for them ahead of time. How can you and your family be ready for an emergency? What things would you need? The list on the next page can help.

Emergency Checklist

☑ When lights go out, **flashlights** come in handy. Don't forget extra **batteries!**

☑ Turn on a **battery-powered radio.** No, not for music. Listen for warnings and emergency information.

☑ Store plenty of **canned goods** so you'll have something to eat! "Arf! Arf!" Don't forget, pets get hungry too!

☑ Remember, you can't open a can without a **can opener!**

☑ Sip! Gulp! Be sure to get lots of **water.**

☑ The doctor might not be in so make sure you've got **medicine** and **bandages.**

☑ Pack **clothes, blankets,** and **pillows.** You'll want to be comfortable.

4 YOU 2 DO

Word Play

Pick a natural disaster. Write its name on a sheet of paper. Then jot down as many words as you can make from the letters in the word. Have a contest with a friend to see who can make the most words.

Making Connections

Get a partner. Choose two natural disasters you read about. Talk about how these disasters are alike and how they are different. Then make a chart with two columns. In one column list how the disasters are alike. In the other column list how they are different.

On Paper

Do you and your family have a plan for an emergency? If you do, tell what it is. If you don't have a plan, write one. Share the plan with your family.

Glossary

dis·cov·er (dis kuv´ ər), *VERB.* to find out something that was not known before: *He discovered tiny insects living under the stone.* **dis·cov·ered, dis·cov·er·ing.**

el·e·phant (el´ ə fənt), *NOUN.* a very large mammal: *An elephant has large ears and a long trunk.*

e·mer·gen·cy (i mėr´ jən sē), *NOUN.* a situation that calls for immediate action: *In an emergency dial 911.* *PL.* **e·mer·gen·cies.**

en·dan·gered (en dān´ jərd), *ADJECTIVE.* at risk of no longer existing: *Giant pandas are endangered animals.*

ex·plain (ek splān´), *VERB.* to tell about something so that people are able to understand it: *The teacher explained multiplication to the class.* **ex·plained, ex·plain·ing.**

ex·tinct (ek stingkt´), *ADJECTIVE.* no longer existing: *Dinosaurs are extinct.*

a	in hat	ō	in open	sh	in she
ā	in age	ȯ	in all	th	in thin
â	in care	ô	in order	ᴛH	in then
ä	in far	oi	in oil	zh	in measure
e	in let	ou	in out		a in about
ē	in equal	u	in cup		e in taken
ėr	in term	u̇	in put	ə=	i in pencil
i	in it	ü	in rule		o in lemon
ī	in ice	ch	in child		u in circus
o	in hot	ng	in long		

flood (flud), *NOUN.* a great flow of water over an area that is usually dry land: *The heavy rains caused a flood.*

flow·er (flou´ ər), *NOUN.* a part of a plant or tree that produces the seed; blossom: *My favorite flower is a rose.*

grow (grō), *VERB.* to become bigger: *Plants grow from seeds.* **grew, grow·ing, grown.**

hur·ri·cane (hėr´ ə kān), *NOUN.* a fierce storm with very strong, dangerous winds and, usually, very heavy rain: *The wind in a hurricane blows at more than 75 miles per hour.*

myth (mith), *NOUN.* a legend or story, usually one that attempts to explain something in nature: *According to Greek myth, the god Zeus used lightning as a weapon.*

nat·ur·al (nach´ ər əl), *ADJECTIVE.* not artificial; not made by human beings: *Coal and oil are natural products.*

a in hat	ō in open	sh in she
ā in age	ȯ in all	th in thin
â in care	ô in order	ŦH in then
ä in far	oi in oil	zh in measure
e in let	ou in out	a in about
ē in equal	u in cup	e in taken
ėr in term	u̇ in put	ə = i in pencil
i in it	ü in rule	o in lemon
ī in ice	ch in child	u in circus
o in hot	ng in long	

na·ture (nā´ chər), NOUN. everything in the world not made by people: *Plants, animals, air, water, mountains, and people are parts of nature.*

ob·serve (əb zėrv´), VERB. to look at something carefully in order to learn about it; study: *Astronomers observe the stars.* **ob·served, ob·serv·ing.**

res·cue (res´ kyü), VERB. to save someone or something from danger, capture, or harm; free; deliver: *The dog was rescued from danger.* **res·cued, res·cu·ing.**

scat·ter (skat´ ər), *VERB.* to throw a little bit of something here and some more over there; sprinkle: *Let's scatter salt on the sidewalk to melt the ice.* **scat·tered, scat·ter·ing.**

sci·en·tist (sī´ ən tist), *NOUN.* a person who studies a science: *A scientist tries to find out why things are the way they are.*

sense (sens), *NOUN.* a power of a living thing to know what happens outside itself; sight, smell, taste, hearing, and touch are the physical senses: *A dog has a very keen sense of smell.*

a in hat	ō in open	sh in she
ā in age	ȯ in all	th in thin
â in care	ô in order	ᴛʜ in then
ä in far	oi in oil	zh in measure
e in let	ou in out	⎧ a in about
ē in equal	u in cup	⎪ e in taken
ėr in term	u̇ in put	ə = ⎨ i in pencil
i in it	ü in rule	⎪ o in lemon
ī in ice	ch in child	⎩ u in circus
o in hot	ng in long	

sight (sīt), NOUN.

> 1 the power or sense of seeing: *We know what things look like through our sense of sight.*
>
> 2 thing seen; view; glimpse: *I can't stand the sight of blood.*

soil (soil), NOUN. the top layer of the Earth; dirt: *They planted flowers in rich soil.*

taste (tāst),

> 1 NOUN. the power to take in the flavor that things have: *The taste of sugar is sweet.*
>
> 2 VERB. to find out whether something is sweet, sour, salty, or bitter when you put it in your mouth: *You taste things with your tongue.* **tast·ed, tast·ing.**

touch (tuch),

    1 *NOUN.* the power by which a person knows about things by feeling or handling them: *Touch is one of the five senses.*

    2 *VERB.* to be next to; come up against: *Your sleeve is touching the butter.* **touched, touch·ing.**

van·ish (van´ ish), *VERB.* to disappear suddenly: *The sun vanished behind a cloud.* **van·ished, van·ish·ing.**

veg·e·ta·ble (vej´ tə bəl or vej´ ə tə bəl), *NOUN.* a plant that has fruit, seeds, leaves, roots, or other parts used for food: *Peas, lettuce, beets, and zucchini are vegetables.*

warn·ing (wôr´ ning), *NOUN.* notice given in advance: *The siren was a warning that a fire truck was coming.*

a in hat	ō in open	sh in she
ā in age	ȯ in all	th in thin
â in care	ô in order	ᵺ in then
ä in far	oi in oil	zh in measure
e in let	ou in out	a in about
ē in equal	u in cup	e in taken
ėr in term	ù in put	ə = i in pencil
i in it	ü in rule	o in lemon
ī in ice	ch in child	u in circus
o in hot	ng in long	

Acknowledgments

Text

28 Recipe for "Frittata" from *The Edible Schoolyard*, Martin Luther King Jr. Middle School, Berkeley, CA. Used by permission of Chez Panisse Foundation.

Illustrations

Opener: Gary Torrisi; **20–26** Mercedes McDonald; **28–29** Patt Dalby; **34, 36** Beatrice Willey; **36** Robert (Bob) Kayganich; **38** Matt Zang; **54** Felipe Ugalde; **60–63** Laura Freeman-Hines; **72–79** Karen Lee; **86, 98, 100–104** Gary Torrisi; **106** Steven Mach; **110, 124–131** Amy Huntington

Photographs

Every effort has been made to secure permission and provide appropriate credit for photographic material. The publisher deeply regrets any omission and pledges to correct errors called to its attention in subsequent editions.

Unless otherwise acknowledged, all photographs are the property of Scott Foresman, a division of Pearson Education.

Photo locators denoted as follows: Top (T), Center (C), Bottom (B), Left (L), Right (R), Background (Bkgd).

Opener: (BR) ©WizData, Inc./Alamy, ©Frans Lanting/Minden Pictures, (L) ©Jim Boorman/Getty Images; **1** ©Kenneth Garrett/National Geographic Image Collection; **2** (TR) ©Stockbyte, (CL) ©Robert Pickett/Alamy Images, (BL) ©Annie Griffiths Belt/Corbis; **3** (T) ©Tom Vezo/Nature Picture Library, (BR) Getty Images; **5** (BL, C) ©Royalty-Free/Corbis; **6** ©Stockbyte; **7** ©WizData, Inc./Alamy; **8** (C) ©Sean Justice/Getty Images, (TR) ©Stockbyte; **9** ©Tom Stewart/Corbis; **10** ©Todd Gipstein/National Geographic Image Collection; **11** (BR) ©WizData, Inc./Alamy, (T) ©Dennis Frates/Alamy Images; **13** ©Mary Evans Picture Library/Alamy Images; **14** ©Gianni Dagli Orti/Corbis; **15** ©Lynsey Addario/Corbis; **16** Thomas Jefferson Foundation, Inc.; **17** Robert C. Lautman/©Thomas Jefferson Foundation, Inc.; **18** Chelsea Chapmen/©The Edible Schoolyard; **19** Chelsea Chapman/©The Edible Schoolyard; **28** Chelsea Chapman/©The Edible Schoolyard; **31** (C, T) Getty Images; **32** (CR) ©Heather Angel/Alamy Images, (TR) ©Robert Pickett/Alamy Images, (BR) ©Maximilian Weinzierl/Alamy Images; **33** (TL) ©Blickwinkel/Alamy Images, (BR) ©Royalty-Free/Corbis; **35** ©Studio Photogram/Alamy; **37** ©Pete Turner/Getty Images; **38** (C) BananaStock, (Bkgd) ©Richard Hamilton Smith/Corbis; **40** (TR) ©Royalty-Free/Corbis, (BL, BR) ©Gary Vestal/Getty Images, (Bkgd) Getty Images; **41** (BR, BL) ©Gary Vestal/Getty Images, (Bkgd) Getty Images, (CR) ©Royalty-Free/Corbis; **42** (CL) Getty Images, (R) ©Konard Zelazowski/Alamy Images, (Bkgd) ©Dietrich Rose/Getty Images; **43** ©Johner/Getty Images; **44** (BC) ©Jason Edwards/National Geographic Image Collection, (Bkgd) ©Richard Hamilton Smith/Corbis, (TL) Getty Images; **45** ©Darrell Gulin/Getty Images; **46** (Bkgd, B) Getty Images; **47** (C) ©A. Riedmiller/Peter Arnold, Inc., (Bkgd) Getty Images; **48** (Bkgd) Jupiter Images, (C) ©Arne Pastoor/Getty Images; **49** (C) ©Richard T. Nowitz/Corbis, (Bkgd) Getty Images; **50** (B) ©Annie Griffiths Belt/Corbis, (CR) ©Barry Rosenthal/Getty Images, (CL) ©Heather Angel/Alamy Images, (Bkgd) Getty Images; **51** ©Pixtal/SuperStock; **52** (CL) Getty Images, (B) ©Brownie Harris/Corbis; **53** ©Paul & Lindamarie Ambrose/Getty Images; **56** (TC) ©Robert Pickett/Alamy Images, (TL) ©Blickwinkel/Alamy Images, (CL) ©Zave Smith/Getty Images; **57** ©Glowimages/Getty Images; **58** (TR) ©Stefano Bianchetti/Corbis, (TCR) Getty Images, (TR) ©Royalty-Free/Corbis; **64** (TL) ©Stefano Bianchetti/Corbis, (TL) Getty Images; **65** (TR) ©Mary Evans Picture Library/Alamy Images, (TR) ©Alinari Archives/Corbis, (Bkgd) ©O. Louis Mazzatenta/Getty Images; **66** (CL) ©Bettmann/Corbis, (C) Getty Images, (TR) DAJ/Getty Images, (T) ©Martin Ruegner/Getty Images; **67** (T) Getty Images, (C) ©Blend Images/Getty Images, (TR) DAJ/Getty Images; **68** (CL) Corbis, (TL) Getty Images, (T) ©Wilmar Photography/Alamy Images; **70** (C) Stockdisc, (T) ©Eyebyte/Alamy, (TL) NASA; **71** ©Bill Bachmann/Alamy Images; **80** (TL, TCL) ©Joe McDonald/Corbis, (TCR) ©Gavriel Jecan/Corbis, (BR) ©Sigrid Oisson/Getty Images; **81** (T) ©George D. Lepp/Corbis, (TR) ©Arthur Morris/Corbis; **82** (TL) ©Arthur Morris/Corbis, (BR) Getty Images; **83** Thinkstock; **84** ©Frans Lanting/Minden Pictures, **87** (TL) ©Tom Vezo/Nature Picture Library, (TR) ©C. C. Lockwood/Animals Animals/Earth Scenes; **88** ©Tom Brownold; **89** (TL) ©Joel Sartore/National Geographic Image Collection, (BC) ©Kenneth W. Fink/Photo Researchers, Inc.; **90** (TL) ©Stuart Westmorland/Getty Images, (B) ©Steven J. Kazlowski/Alamy Images; **92** (Bkgd) ©Tom Brakefield/Corbis, (CL) ©Sukree Sukplang/Corbis; **93** ©Kenneth Garrett/National Geographic Image Collection; **94** ©David A. Northcutt/Corbis; **95** ©Frans Lanting/Corbis; **96** (B) ©Heather Angel/Alamy Images, (TR) ©Steve Bloom/Alamy Images, (BL) ©Frans Lanting/Minden Pictures; **108** ©Kenneth Garrett/National Geographic Image Collection; **109** ©Howard Berman/Getty Images; **110** ©Roger Ressmeyer/Corbis; **111** (BC) Getty Images, (T) Corbis; **112** (BR) ©Jeff Greenberg/Veer, Inc., (TC) ©Annie Griffiths/National Geographic Image Collection; **113** (BR) ©Martin Meyer/Corbis, (TC) ©Cameron Davidson/Jupiter Images; **114** ©Roger Ressmeyer/Corbis; **115** (C) ©Scott Olsen/Getty Images, (R) ©John Burcham/Getty Images; **116** ©Randy Wells/Corbis; **118** ©Jim Zuckerman/Corbis; **119** (TR) ©Royalty-Free/Corbis, (TL) ©Martyn Goddaed/Corbis, (BL) ©Chris Collins/Corbis; **120** ©Will & Deni McIntyre/Corbis; **121** ©Michael Pole/Corbis; **122** (BL) ©Chris Carroll/Corbis, (CR) ©Jim Reed/Corbis, (C) ©Matthias Kulka/Corbis, (BR) ©H&S Production/Corbis; **132** (BL) ©Rob Lewine/Corbis, (Bkgd) ©John Sevigny/Corbis; **133** (TL, CL, BL) ©Royalty-Free/Corbis, (CR) ©G. Schuster/Corbis, (CR) H&S Production/Corbis, (TR) Corbis, (CR) ©Larry Williams/Corbis, (BR) ©Ute Kaiser/Corbis; **134** ©Corbis; **136** ©Kenneth Garrett/National Geographic Image Collection; **137** ©Heather Angel/Alamy Images; **138** ©Cameron Davidson/Jupiter Images; **139** ©John Sevigny/Corbis; **140** Thinkstock; **141** Getty Images; **142** ©Sean Justice/Getty Images; **143** ©Tom Stewart/Corbis